How to Be Your Daughter's Daddy

365 WAYS
TO SHOW HER YOU CARE

DAN BOLIN

© 1993 by Dan Bolin
All rights reserved. No part of this publication may be
    reproduced in any form without written permission
    from Piñon Press, P. O. Box 35007, Colorado Springs,
    CO 80935.
Library of Congress Catalog Card Number:
    92-63218
ISBN 08910-97279

Fourth printing, 1994

Printed in the United States of America

*To Cay Bolin,
the best mom
daughters could hope for*

INTRODUCTION

❖

Daughters are great. I love it when one of my daughters puts her hand in mine, when she hugs so tight my neck hurts, when she crawls up onto my lap, or when she whispers a secret in my ear.

I doubt if I would have realized how great daughters are had life been normal.

On Halloween day 1985, my wife, Cay, and I took our two daughters to the doctor. At the time, Catie was age four, and Haley was six weeks old. It was time for a routine checkup. Catie was dressed as Wonder Woman, and Haley was in a cute little pumpkin outfit, complete with a hat that looked like a stem. Dr. Bates was in a Mickey Mouse costume, and Dr. Rogers was dressed as a clown. We had planned a picnic after the visit to the doctor.

Pokes, probes, questions, tests, and within a few minutes we learned that Catie had leukemia.

We were in Dallas at Children's Medical Center in a matter of hours. Tapes played, "I'll cast all my cares upon him." The staff at Children's was in costume as well. We were met by pumpkins, tubes of toothpaste, and pirates.

Friends and family surrounded us. Drs. Kamen, Sartain, Sanders, and Buchanan offered reasonable, rational, and cautious optimism. Catie found that the pills tasted horrible. We tried to sneak them to her in grape juice, apricot preserves, ice cream, and finally in her favorite, macaroni and cheese. Eventually, we discovered that pulverizing the pills and mixing them in chocolate syrup was the only way she could get them down.

Every day became a challenge. Following schedules for pills, shots, tests, and treatments. Protecting her, as best we could, from runny noses and unwashed hands. Acting calm and confident in the face of our own fears and anxiety.

Every day became an adventure. There was so much to

learn—hours in the library, phone calls, medical journals. Could Cay and I keep Catie positive and free from the terror that was our constant companion?

Every day became a gift. We never knew if this birthday party would be her last, if this would be our last vacation, or if this would be Catie's last time to see her beloved Dallas Mavericks play basketball.

People were great. Joe and Claudia Hesh (whose daughter Cori is still winning her fight with leukemia) shared insights, prayers, diet Cokes, and how to work the hospital microwave. Ken and Jan Sutterfield were our friends in need—good friends indeed. The general manager of the Mavericks, Norm Sonju, provided front-row seats, autographed basketballs, and encouragement. President George Bush got on his knees to talk directly to Catie. Barbara Bush sent letters and love. Debbie Dalton, whose son was in Catie's Sunday school class, read stories to her long distance. Pastor Bill Bryan came to Fort Worth to give her a trumpet serenade while she was in two months of isolation.

Bernard King took time to sign an autograph while riding up an elevator after his team (the Washington Bullets) had been beaten by forty points. He had no idea the six-year-old would begin a bone marrow transplant the next day. John Weber and Jim Sundberg got Catie tickets to see the Texas Rangers play the Red Sox in Fenway Park. Owens Elementary was a second family. Mrs. Gazette, Mrs. Weisinger, Mrs. Hall, and Mrs. Ellis were much more than educators. They were her friends. There were countless acts of love from grandparents, other family members, and friends.

While Catie was the focus of our attention, Haley was becoming the life of the party. She had no way of processing what was happening around her, but she learned how to be a helper as she was a part of shots, finger sticks, bone marrow exams, and spinal taps. She went where we went.

We tried very hard to make Haley's life as special as possible. Cay kept a bag of small wrapped toys—ready to balance things when a gift would come for Catie. Catie's schedule dictated the schedule for all of us, but we tried to give Haley some areas of control as well. She could make choices about her blanket, her pacifier, and her dolls.

I rarely traveled without the family. We loved long car trips because they maximized our time together. We drove from East Texas to Los Angeles, Chicago, Boston, and Washington, D.C. Each trip was a challenge, an adventure, and a gift.

Tubes ran in and out of Catie's body. Remission to relapse . . . remission to relapse took its toll on all of us. The strategies of the best minds, the longings of the warmest hearts, and the prayers of the most devoted souls came to an end on Halloween day 1990.

This book is a collection of ideas that I used during those days and ideas that I still use two years later. Haley is seven. She is no longer known as Catie's little sister.

I learned a lot from Catie. I hope Haley has a better daddy because of what I learned.

There are no perfect daddies. We are all busy, we all say the wrong things, and we all struggle trying to know what in the world to do with our daughters. We were never little girls.

Our daughters need us to teach them what true love and affection really are so that they will be able to recognize the counterfeits when they appear. They need to know that they are special. This can happen only as they become a priority in our lives. We have a responsibility to protect, direct, and correct their lives and to do it in the most loving, strong, and joyful manner possible.

British author C. S. Lewis, in his classic book *The Lion, the Witch and the Wardrobe*, details the adventures of four children who become kings and queens in the fantasy land of Narnia. A wise old professor believes the children's tale of adventure. In the final page of the book, he reassures them by saying, "Once a king (or queen) in Narnia, always a king (or queen) in Narnia." As fathers, we have the privilege of lighting a flame of queenly character in our daughters that no trauma, hardship, or criticism can ever snuff out.

The worth that your daughter sees in herself will be derived from the image that you project to her, and that takes time. The only quality time that you will enjoy with your daughter is what flows from the quantity of time you invest with her. I hope that this little book gives you a lot of ideas that work as you become the very best daddy your daughter could ever have.

1

Learn the names of her dolls or stuffed animals.

❖

2

Surprise her by celebrating her "half birthday."

❖

3

Make a thin layer of Jell-O and carve it
into letters, numbers, figures, etc.

4

Together, write a family newspaper
for friends and relatives.

❖

5

Keep a lot of pictures of her in your wallet.

❖

6

Take a walk together with a memento bag
and collect interesting leaves, rocks, or junk.

7
Read, read, read to her.

8
Kiss her mother in her presence.

9
Give her privacy when
she is talking to her dolls.

10
Take her to the bank
and open a savings account.

11
With a pattern of her foot, make dozens
of footprints out of construction paper.
Leave them in a trail to a special, simple prize
or gift, hidden in your home.

12
Design your family Christmas card together.

❖

13
Brush her hair.

❖

14
Give her a set of keys to your home.

15
Help her make a bug cage.

❖

16
Help her catch a bug for her bug cage.

❖

17
Eat lunch with her at her school.

18
Teach her to weave a ring out of grass.

❖

19
Let her paint graffiti on the walls of her room
two days before it is repainted.

❖

20
Make her an admiral's hat out of newspaper.

21
Paint a "HAPPY BIRTHDAY" banner for her.

❖

22
Tell her that the dress is pretty because it is on her.

❖

23
Buy her ten shares of stock in an inexpensive
company that she will recognize
and watch it make or lose money.

24
Help her look up new words in a dictionary.

❖

25
Teach her how to blow up and pop a bag.

❖

26
Get her bed two more pillows than it needs.

27

Pretend to be an animal in the circus
and let her be the ringmaster.

❖

28

Take her fishing.

❖

29

Use a globe to locate friends, travel destinations,
and current events together.

30
Take her on a sound scavenger hunt
with a tape recorder.

❖

31
Give her a secondhand suitcase
full of secondhand dress-up clothes.

❖

32
Work together to make a collage of her life
with pictures cut from magazines.

33

Agree on a secret code word or phrase for
"It's time to go home" to use in public.
(She says, "Daddy, you need to polish your shoes,"
and I say, "I am going
to polish them very soon," or
"I can't polish them for a while.")

34

Listen to classical music in the car.

35
Show her how to make giant soap bubbles.

❖

36
Plan a vacation together—imaginary or real.

❖

37
Give her several trinkets on her birthday
and wrap each one individually.

38
Send her a flower when you are out of town.

❖

39
Hang a picture she has drawn on a wall at work.

❖

40
Buy her new crayons and a coloring book
for a special event where she will need
to be extra good and especially quiet.

41
While traveling,
pretend that horses are called "cows"
and cows are called "horses."
Let her try to get you to realize your mistake.

42
Leave her a note or present
where she will find it when you are out of town
or not home when she goes to sleep.

43

Together, roast miniature marshmallows
with toothpicks over the flame of a candle.

44

Learn a simple magic trick to amaze her
and her friends.

45
Keep a plastic dinosaur
in the glove compartment of your car
for a special treat on a long trip.

46
When returning from a routine trip to the store,
take an unusual turn that will lengthen the drive.
When she asks why, explain that you want
more time to be with her.

47
Ask her to help you put air in the tires of your car.

48
Show her your picture
in your high school yearbook.

49
Read all of the information her teacher sends home
from school and comment on it to her.

50
Help her paint an original T-shirt
for a special occasion.

❖

51
Take her for a walk
through a hardware store
and explain the function
of various tools.

52

Compliment her character and skill three times for every one compliment on her appearance.

❖

53

Help her learn directions while you drive. Ask her "Right, left, or straight?" at each intersection.

❖

54

On a one-foot square of grass, find all the living things that are visible in that space.

55

Play "Twenty Questions." One person thinks
of a person, place, or thing while the other
asks yes-or-no questions to get clues.
Only twenty questions per item.

56

Estimate distances to interesting points.
Take a walk and stretch a hundred-foot rope
between yourselves as many times as it takes
until you reach the estimated point.

57

Spend a half hour looking through
a toy catalog with her.

❖

58

Order pencils with her name on them.

❖

59

On her birthday, ask her to lie on butcher paper,
and trace around her. Repeat the process each year
to show her how much she has grown.

60
Teach her to count to ten in a foreign language.

---❖---

61
Ask her to tell you three words that describe people she knows. Talk about the words.

---❖---

62
Take her on a train ride.

63

Give her three piggy banks for her money.
Use one for "save," one for "spend,"
and one for "give."

64

Join her school's parent association.

65

Volunteer at her school.

66
Expect obedience.

❖

67
When traveling in two cars, use an inexpensive set
of walkie-talkies to chat back and forth.

❖

68
Give up something for her (golf, television,
smoking, etc.). She may not appreciate it,
but it will remind you of her great worth to you.

69
Take her with you when you play golf.

70
Get to know people very, very well before you allow
her to spend the night at someone's home.
Explain to her your behavioral expectations
before she is allowed to accept an invitation.

71
Encourage her to try out for a play.

72

Take her to a girls' volleyball or basketball game
at the high school she will attend.

73

Play "City or State?" Name a city or state,
then she tells you which it is.

74

Choose videos for her to watch
rather than TV programing.

75

Write a letter to her for New Year's Day.
Tell her what you've noticed about her
in the last year.

❖

76

String popcorn for your Christmas tree.

❖

77

Teach her to call 911 if there is an emergency.

78

Encourage her to memorize
a short proverb, such as,
"A cheerful heart is good medicine."

79

Explain to her the significance
of Jewish holidays,
so she will understand other traditions.
(Choose any religion that is not your own.)

80
Tell her you are sorry when you hurt her feelings.

81
Hold her when she cries.

82
Help her write her own thank-you notes.

83

Play games with her that require thinking
rather than just chance.

❖

84

Have an art show of her masterpieces.
Invite your friends and relatives to come
and buy original, signed art work.
Set low prices so everything will sell.

85
When she wants a dog,
give her a hamster.

86
When she takes good care
of her hamster,
give her a dog.

87

Encourage her to practice
filling out applications
for everything. While you wait at banks,
restaurants, and department stores,
she can be learning her full name,
address, and phone number.

❖

88

Make sure she goes
to religious services.

89
Make sure you go with her
to religious services.

90
Work with her on activities
for Girl Scouts and church.

91
Let her have any loose change
that she finds in your home.

92
Have some of her schoolwork laminated.

93
Help her make homemade potpourri
with dried flower petals.

94
Make a list of all the people who love her.

95
Make a list of the people she loves.

96
Find out what she likes
and doesn't like on her hamburgers.

97
Know her favorite color.

98
Get a picture of the children in her school class and learn their names.

❖

99
Give her her very own tape player so she can fall asleep listening to music or stories.

❖

100
Keep crayons in your office so she can visit and have something to do.

101
Get her a small tape measure.
Guess how long things are,
then see which of you guessed closer.

102
Tell her Bible stories.

103
Get a book of dates and tell her about interesting
things that happened on that day.

104
Help her draw a picture book
of a story you have told her.

105
Look through a clothing catalog
and ask her what she likes and doesn't like.

106
Look through a clothing catalog
and explain to her what is becoming
on a young lady and what is not.

107
Ask her to help you wash the car.

108
Explore the attic together.

109
Make sock puppets with unmatched white socks.
Draw faces with markers.

110
Paint a special message for her mother
on a wooden cutting board.

111
Make a calendar of the big events of her year.

112

Make sure her winter coat is her favorite color,
so she will be more likely to wear it
on the marginally cold days.

❖

113

Get dressed up and take her to high tea
one afternoon at a nice restaurant.

114
Give her a coupon for you
to make her bed one day.

115
Teach her to make an angel pattern
by lying in the snow.

116
Make a snowman together.

117
Memorize the names
of past presidents with her.

118
Call her from work when she gets home
from school just to see how her day went.

119
After you both decide what you will order
at a restaurant, guess what the other selected.

120
Help her interview her grandparents
and other relatives on a tape recorder.

❖

121
Write a poem about her
and read it to her on a special occasion.

❖

122
Put bread out for the birds with her.

123
Pray for her future husband.

124
Help her keep a journal
of a family trip or vacation.

125
Look through a book of house plans with her
and ask her to pick her dream house.

126
Stop and read
the historical markers to her.

127
Give her her own measuring cups
to play with while learning volumes.

128

Take her to the library and check out
the books that were your favorites
when you were her age.

129

Help her write a letter to the author
of a book she really likes.

130
Visit a children's museum together.

❖

131
Read the weather report for cities
around the country where her relatives
or friends live.

❖

132
Buy her a rubber stamp of her name and address.

133

Let her personalize the cover plate
on the light switch in her room with paint.

❖

134

Take her to volunteer with you at a food bank.

❖

135

Always count the railroad cars
when you see a train.

136
Ask her to help you pump gas.

137
Help her clean her room.

138
Get personalized stationery for her.

139

Buy or make a small trophy for her
when she has a major accomplishment.

140

Buy her a single red rose and take her on a "date."

141

Let her take her own pictures. Get an inexpensive
camera for her own, or let her use
a roll of film in your camera.

142
Help her start a coin collection.

143
Help her start a stamp collection.

144
Help her start a baseball card collection
(unless she likes football
or basketball better!).

145

Write her a letter praising an accomplishment
in her life or a character trait
you want to reinforce.

146

Surprise her!
Pick her up from school
and stop for ice cream on the way home.

147

Make plaster of Paris trinkets together.
Paint them and glue magnets on the back.
Give them as gifts for your
friends' and relatives' refrigerators.

❖

148

Make up stories to tell her at bedtime.
Develop regular characters
to repeat in every story.

149

Get a book on animal tracks and explore
a pond or a trail together
to see what animals live in the area.

❖

150

Play "Captain of Captivity."
Hug her so she can't get away. Then pretend
to fall asleep and allow her to get free
before you "awake" to capture her again.

151
Ask her to help you rake leaves
(or pine needles).

❖

152
Put her in a garbage can full of leaves
and carry her in the garbage can.

❖

153
Shop together for a gift for her mom.

154
Fly a kite with her.

❖

155
While waiting for service in a restaurant, place
a fork and knife in any arrangement.
Tell her that it is a code for a number
from zero to ten. Let her guess the number.
In reality, the code is how many fingers
you have on the table. Do this several times;
she'll figure it out.

156
Tell her stories about when you were her age.

---❖---

157
Help her plant and tend a garden.

---❖---

158
Put a pine cone in water for several minutes
and watch it close. Allow it to dry
for a few days and watch it open.
(You can speed the process in a microwave.)

159

Put colored water in a two-liter bottle.
Connect another to it like an hourglass
and turn it over. Give it a swirl
and you will create a tornado in a bottle.

❖

160

"Collect" license plates from as many states
as possible when traveling.
Get a map of the United States and mark through
a state when the plate has been seen.

161

Go on a camera scavenger hunt together.
Make a list of things that you want pictures of.
On your adventure, stop and take pictures
of those objects.

162

Use a highlighter to track your progress
on a map when you travel.

163
Visit a zoo together.

164
Play "Add an Adjective."
Pick any object and begin by naming one
characteristic, such as it is "tall."
She adds a characteristic—it is "tall and green."
See how many adjectives you can use to describe
the object before one of you forgets the order.

165
Meet the principal at her school.

166
Buy cars with bench seats in front
so that she can sit next to you.

167
As a family,
see "The Nutcracker" every Christmas.

168
Teach her a big word.

169
Set up recycling bags in your home to be good
stewards of what God has entrusted to you.

170
Give her a small present to open
during siblings' birthday parties.

171
Find a way for her to ride a pony.

172
Always sign her report card
and talk about it with her.
Make sure she knows that you love her
no matter what grades she brings home.

173
Encourage her to tape record messages
to send to grandparents and loved ones
who do not live nearby.

174
Freeze Kool-Aid in a sterile rubber glove
or large plastic bag to make a giant Popsicle.

175
Give her a personalized gift each Christmas.

176

Don't let your home get too clean. She needs
to grow up in a place that is low on stress.

❖

177

Don't display valuable, breakable items
in your home. She will inevitably bump and break
one. The pain and guilt are not worth it.
Your home can become a museum
after she is grown.

178
A few times a year,
make a quick run to the yogurt store together
after what should be bedtime.

179
Take time to talk with her in her room
before she falls asleep.

180

Create a time line of major events
in world history. Put the pictures up
around the walls of her room.

181

Help her stencil a border pattern
around the top of her walls.

182

Create a time line of the events
of your family history. Show her all the
significant events that concern her.

❖

183

Go on a newspaper scavenger hunt.
Give her a list of ten to twenty items to find
in the newspaper (weather, a baseball player,
ad for toothpaste, etc.). See how long
it takes her to find the items on the list.

184

At Thanksgiving, list ten to fifteen things
you are most thankful for about her.

❖

185

Around Christmas, have a "Jesus' Birthday Party."
Invite her friends, eat cake,
read the Christmas story from the Bible,
and exchange small presents.

186

Read biographies of people who did
great things and let her know
that they were no different from her.

❖

187

Take her to see the President or Vice-President
when he is in your area.

188
Cook "breakfast in bed" together for her mom.

❖

189
Go with her to doctor's appointments.

❖

190
Wake her up gently and slowly—*always*.

191

Make a weather board. Put a few hooks
on a small board. Prepare tags with numbers
and a few key words.
Let her hang the temperature
and weather condition
each morning before school.

192

Ask her how her dolls
or stuffed animals are doing.

193
Let her enjoy an imaginary friend.

❖

194
Make candles in plastic communion cups.
Tie a string wick to a toothpick.
Place the toothpick across the top
of the container so the end
of the wick touches the bottom.
Pour in melted wax. When the wax cools,
clip the wick from the toothpick
and enjoy your mini-candle.

195

Visit a cemetery
and talk about our bodies
as homes where we live for a while.
Explain that death is like moving out
of this home into a new home
that God has prepared for us in heaven.

❖

196

Give her lots of hugs.

197
Color pictures with her. Use as many colors
as possible and try to stay within the lines!

198
Run through the sprinkler with her.

199
Find a four-leaf clover with her.
Dry it in a book for her to keep.

200
Teach her to use a computer.

201
Take her to select and cut your Christmas tree.

202
Finger paint with chocolate,
lemon, or strawberry pudding.

203
Make eye contact with her
when you talk to her.

204
Make mini-pizzas, using English muffins
topped with pizza sauce, cheese,
and slices of pepperoni.

205
Visit a school board
or city council meeting together.

206
Ask her to select one of her toys
that is in good working order
to give to charity.

207
Use an Advent calendar
during the weeks before Christmas.

208
Make maracas by covering light bulbs
with layers of papier-mâché.
When they dry, gently break the glass
and paint them.

209
Practice a fire drill in your home.
Warn everyone first.

210
Help her write your representative in Congress
about an issue that is important to her.

211
Never allow her to ride
in the back of a pickup truck.

212

Give her a quarter every time she catches
you driving without using your seat belt.

❖

213

Press leaves in a dictionary.

❖

214

Whistle the story of the three bears.
Use tone and volume changes
along with gestures to tell the story.

215

Ask her for a "date" that includes dinner
at her favorite fast-food restaurant
and an activity she really enjoys.

216

Stop for donut holes
on the way to or from
a family outing.

217

Take her bowling to an alley that has
an inflatable tube placed in the gutters,
so that pins are knocked down
every time she rolls the ball.

218

Help her have a garage sale
of her old toys and clothes.

219

When her clothes are monogrammed
only use her initials. (Displaying her name
can allow an unscrupulous person
to gain her confidence.)

❖

220

Send her a card or letter
the day before you go out of town,
so that she will receive it right after you leave.

221
Work on jigsaw puzzles with her.

222
The next time you play Monopoly,
make sure she is able to buy
Park Place and Boardwalk.

223

Make a family time capsule. Include a letter
about your family, a few coins,
the front page of a newspaper,
pictures, and a list of current prices. Bury it
where you can find it again in a few years.

224

When you move into a new home, plant a tree
as a reminder of how long you've lived there.

225
Coach her T-ball team.

❖

226
Check out a tree identification book
from the library and discover which ones
are in your neighborhood.

❖

227
Using the letters from a long word,
see how many smaller words you can each create.

228

Make a "worm squirm." Remove a paper
straw wrapper by stripping it off into a tight
accordion shape. Teach her to put a drop of water
on the wrapper; watch the wrapper expand,
moving like a worm.

❖

229

Train together and participate
in a one-K fun run.

230
Teach her the difference
between the adjective "good"
and the adverb "well."

231
Get her a marker board and four erasable,
colored markers and draw together.

232

When she's a preteen, take her on a tour
of the county jail.
Talk about the issues this raises.

233

Play "Categories." Select a category such as "cities"
and find words in that category
that start with each letter of the alphabet
(i.e., Atlanta, Boston, Cleveland, etc.).

234
Play balloon basketball in her room,
using a wastebasket as the hoop.

❖

235
Give her her own office supplies—
stapler, tape, ruler, hole punch, scissors, etc.

❖

236
Get her a small, fishing tackle box
to store and carry art supplies.

237

Review her spelling words
over the phone when you are out of town.

❖

238

Let her take her doll or special toy
into the restaurant.

❖

239

Give her her own subscription
to a children's magazine.

240
Role play meeting new people
so she will have more confidence
in what can be threatening situations.

❖

241
Cook breakfast together for the family dinner.

❖

242
Read her books in series
(*Little House, Ramona, Chronicles of Narnia*).

243

Get the card games
"Authors" and "Composers" for her.

244

Invite someone who has lived
in a foreign country over for dinner
to talk about life in that country.

245

Spend time in the children's section of a bookstore.

246
Jump rope with her.

247
Never tell her scary stories.

248
Let her put stickers and decals
on the windows in her room.

249
Go with her to buy a pair of saddle oxfords.

250
Say, "I'm sorry. Please forgive me."

251
Make a personalized ornament together
for your Christmas tree.

252
Make "Slice and Bake"
refrigerator cookies with her.

253
Teach her that police officers are her friends.

254
Paint her fingernails and toenails.

255

Pretend that the car is driving itself. Turn
into a fast-food drive-through
and buy a treat so that the car will let you go on.

256

Take her to hear a chamber music concert.

257

Teach her the names of shapes—
triangles through the ten-sided decagon.

258
Teach her to draw a pig using eighteen circles.

259

Buy her a receipt pad to play waitress at dinner.
She can tell all the family members
what today's special is and bring it to them.
Leave her a nice tip.

260

Enter some of her artwork
in a local county fair.

261
Use a book of names to find the meaning
of her name, your name, and her friends' names.

❖

262
Help her decorate her bicycle so she can ride
in a Fourth of July community parade.

❖

263
Help her draw a hopscotch pattern
on the sidewalk or driveway with chalk.

264

Make her a pair of tin can stilts.
Add long pieces of string so she can hold on
and steady the cans under her shoes.

265

Encourage her to eat
until she is satisfied,
not until she has cleaned her plate.

266

Ask her to draw
a picture of one of her heroes.
Find out why
she picked that person.

267

Make fossils by coating clean,
dry chicken bones
with plaster of Paris.

268

Make paper airplanes.
Launch them by placing them on the blades
of a ceiling fan and turning it on slowly.
(Make sure she understands this is an activity
parents must always be involved in.)

❖

269

Sit near the front at special events or other
public meetings. That way she can see what
is happening and feel more involved.

270
Call broccoli "baby trees."

271
Work simple but challenging
crossword puzzles with her.

272
Read her articles from the newspaper.

273
Smear shaving cream
on the bathroom mirror and draw pictures
together with your fingers.

274
Get her a special night light.

275
Pray with her at bedtime.

276
Teach her to swim.

❖

277
Buy her a life jacket to wear around water.

❖

278
Get her a sandbox
and build a castle with her.

279
Give her some miniature tools
so that she can help you with yardwork.

❖

280
Build a log cabin together
with Popsicle sticks and glue.

❖

281
Let her order a topping
for her frozen yogurt or ice cream.

282

Get her a reading light for her bed.

❖

283

Take her to an Easter sunrise service.

❖

284

Put food coloring
in almost anything
the two of you want to cook.

285
Help her learn the books of the Bible,
in case she's ever on "Jeopardy."

❖

286
Take her to get her sight and hearing checked.

❖

287
Help her clip coupons.
Give her a percentage of what you save.

288
Hold her hand when crossing the street.

❖

289
Teach her that she doesn't have to keep a secret
with any adult except you and her mom.

❖

290
Teach her how explanatory notes
are used in the dictionary.

291

Help her write to a company,
thanking them for a product
that she uses and enjoys.

292

Tour a manufacturing plant together.

293

Watch a potter throwing on a wheel.

294
Go to the hospital to view infants
through the nursery window.

295
Teach her the names of the oceans.

296
Honk when you pull in the driveway
to let her know you are home.
Teach her never to run toward the car.

297

Paint lines on your driveway to indicate
how far she can go
without getting special permission.

298

Point out special times when your
odometer lines up in unusual patterns
or turns another 10,000 miles.

299
Be a chaperone on her school field trips.

❖

300
Visit a religious service of a denomination
that is not your own.

❖

301
Teach her how to avoid giving
too much information over the telephone.

302

Use a magnifying glass together to examine
all kinds of little things.

❖

303

Help her make a tent in her room
with a blanket stretched over chairs and tucked
into dresser drawers.

❖

304

Use one baby-sitter as much as possible.

305
Get her a copy of the front page
of your local newspaper for the day she was born.

306
Teach her to use
the fire extinguisher in your home.

307
Work together to memorize a classic poem.

308
Climb a tree with her.

309
Let her take apart an old toy
or piece of equipment.

310
Squeeze fresh orange juice for her
on Christmas morning, her birthday,
and a few other special days each year.

311
Take her to the park and push her in a swing.

❖

312
Take her on a picnic.

❖

313
Write a one-act play together,
and perform it for your family.

314
Make a list of words that rhyme with her name and use them when possible.

---❖---

315
Draw a family tree for her to keep.

---❖---

316
Ask her to teach you something
that she is good at
(jacks, jumping rope, hopscotch, cooking).

317

On your own, read *The Blessing* by John Trent and Gary Smalley, *Little House on the Freeway* by Tim Kimmel, and *Point Man* by Steve Farrar.

❖

318

Go to the grocery store together and learn what she likes and doesn't like.

❖

319

Tape record her reading a favorite story.

320
Look through your cereal bowls
for the biggest flake, before pouring on milk.

❖

321
Give her a miniature tea service
so that she can have tea parties with her dolls.

❖

322
Tell her about how you met her mother.

323
Take her to visit
the grade school you attended.

324
Get her a children's Bible with her name on it.

325
Take her to visit your state capitol building.

326
Always speak highly of her teachers.

327
Put a bulletin board in her room
to display her pictures, homework,
awards, and certificates.

328
Sing in the car.

329
Buy her scented bubble bath.

330
Keep a book with you so that you can fill
odd moments of time reading to her.

331
Take her to the airport for lunch
and watch the planes take off and land.

332
Put a thermometer
outside her window.

333
Pay a little more for Band-Aids
with bright colors or cartoon characters.
When she needs a Band-Aid,
she needs to feel special.

334

Create a seasonal centerpiece together
for your dinner table
by filling a small basket
with plants and flowers.

335

Teach her the history
and meaning behind
"The Star-Spangled Banner."

336

Lie on your backs outside and look at the sky.
See how many things
you can imagine in the clouds.

337

Lay out the design of a city on your driveway
or patio using chalk or masking tape.

338
Show her photographs or movies
of you as a child.

❖

339
Explain to her why the American flag
has thirteen stripes and fifty stars.

❖

340
Insist that she wear a helmet
when riding a bicycle.

341

Send an "I love you" note
in her lunch box.

342

Put an adjustable-height basketball hoop
in your driveway. Start to play
at about six feet six inches.

343

Test bicycle horns with her at a store.

344
Play "Name That Thing."
Select an object
and take turns naming things
that resemble it.

345
Make a tepee out of three
or four poles and two bed sheets.

346
Roast pumpkin seeds in the oven.

347
Explain to her why you select
the candidates for whom you vote.

348
Tell her she has a beautiful smile.

349

Go to a wedding and talk with her about
the significance of the symbolism (i.e., rings, unity
candle, being married in a church).

❖

350

Put extra money in her backpack, or whatever she
takes to school, so that she will have the security
of a backup if she forgets her lunch money.

351

Make "hoe cakes." Clean a garden hoe
and heat it over an open fire.
Pour pancake batter on the blade of the hoe.
Wait until it begins to "wink," then turn it over
with a spatula and cook the other side.

❖

352

Hold an Olympic figure-skating competition
on a linoleum floor. Together,
demonstrate the artistry of skaters
in your stocking feet.

353
Teach her the planets' names and order.

❖

354
Make corn husk dolls together.

❖

355
Let her see the stars each night by scattering
luminescent paper cut to look like stars
on the ceiling of her room.

356
Help her learn
the names of the continents.

357
Get a poster of the flags
from all the countries in the world.
As various countries come up in conversation
show her the flag of that country.

358

Keep fruit and fruit juice
in your home for snacks.

359

Ask her questions
that cannot be answered "yes" or "no."
Draw her into conversations
with "What did you like best about . . . ?"
or "If you could change . . . ,
what would you do?"

360
Have few rules
but enforce the ones you set.

361
Go to her parent-teacher conferences.

362
Take her to an outdoor concert.

363
Teach her how to use the legend on maps.

❖

364
Volunteer together to ring a bell
for charity at Christmas time.

❖

365
Tell her "I love you!"
as often as she can stand it.